Nature Numbers

HOW MANY DOLPHINS IN A POD?

Counting by 10s

Ruth A. Musgrave

10 20 30 40 50 60 70 80 90 100

Children's Press®
An imprint of Scholastic Inc.

Library of Congress Cataloging-in-Publication Data
Names: Musgrave, Ruth A., 1960- author.
Title: How many dolphins in a pod? : counting by tens /
  Ruth A. Musgrave.
Description: New York : Children's Press, an imprint of Scholastic
  Inc., [2022]. | Series: Nature numbers | Includes index. | Audience:
  Ages 5-7. | Audience: Grades K-1. | Summary: "Nonfiction,
  full-color photos of animals and nature introduce basic math
  concepts and encourage kids to see a world of numbers all
  around them"– Provided by publisher.
Identifiers: LCCN 2021031697 (print) | LCCN 2021031698 (ebook)
  | ISBN 9781338765243 (library binding) | ISBN 9781338765250
  (paperback) | ISBN 9781338771374 (ebk)
Subjects: LCSH: Counting–Juvenile literature. | Arithmetic–Juvenile
  literature. | Animals–Miscellanea–Juvenile literature. | BISAC:
  JUVENILE NONFICTION / General | JUVENILE NONFICTION
  / Mathematics / General
Classification: LCC QA113 .M8856 2022 (print) | LCC QA113
  (ebook) | DDC 513.2/1–dc23
LC record available at https://lccn.loc.gov/2021031697
LC ebook record available at https://lccn.loc.gov/2021031698

First edition, 2022
Series produced by WonderLab Group, LLC
Book design by Moduza Design
Photo editing by Annette Kiesow
Educational consulting by Leigh Hamilton
Copyediting by Jane Sunderland
Proofreading by Molly Reid
Indexing by Connie Binder

Photos ©: cover: art-design-photography.com/Getty Images; back
cover fish: Cynoclub/Dreamstime; 2-3 fish: Cynoclub/Dreamstime;
6-7: cbpix/Getty Images; 9: David Fleetham/Nature Picture Library;
12-13: Rodger Klein/WaterFrame/age fotostock; 16-17: Maieru
Alina/Dreamstime; 22: Doug Perrine/Nature Picture Library;
24: Papilio/Alamy Images; 26-27: Richard Du Toit/Nature
Picture Library.

All other photos © Shutterstock.

To my amazing friend Marsh
—RM

Try It!

Look for answers to all the "Try It!" panels on page 31.

Sharks!

These sleek swimmers lead
the way to the reef . . .

Hurry. Follow those fins.
There are so many animals
to discover and count.

Ten.

Ten hungry sharks search the reef.
Fish is the dish they hope to find.

1

2

3

4

5

6

7

sharks

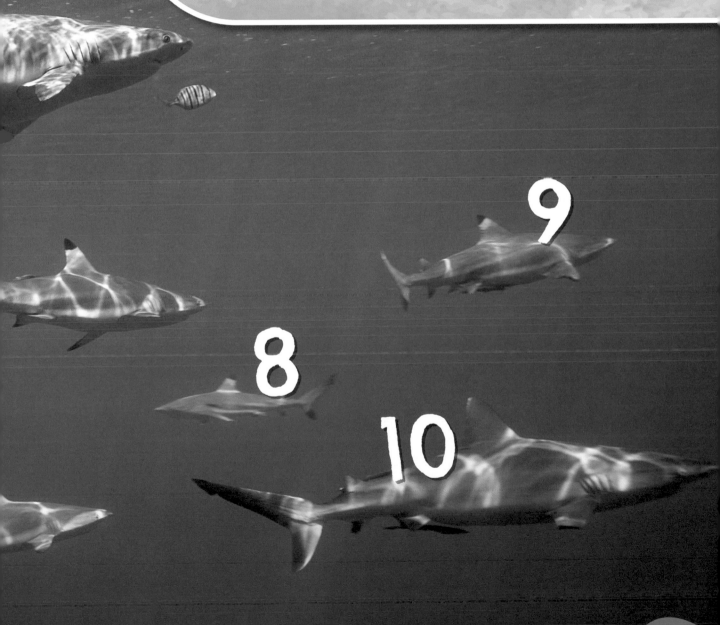

Try It!

Count the sharks one at a time. Can you count them all? How many sharks are there?

9

8

10

Open your arms.

A giant <u>clam</u>'s thick, wavy shell is that big.

Giant clams eat tiny floating plants and animals.

One clam would take up a whole row on a school bus.

Try It!

There are many ways to get to 10.

+ = How many clams?

Let's explore the parts of 10.

giant clam

That tickles.

Clownfish live in an animal called a <u>sea anemone</u>. Its <u>tentacles</u> sting other animals. But not the clownfish. Slime coats a clownfish's skin and protects it from getting stung.

sea anemone

clownfish

Try It!

There are two clownfish in the anemone. What if eight more clownfish visit these two? How many clownfish would there be? Count them.

+ = How many clownfish?

This is another way to get to 10.

**One, two, three sea stars
tiptoe across the rocks.**

They look for dinner to eat.
A sea star pulls its stomach
out of its body to eat.

Then it pulls it back in
when it is full.

sea stars

Try It!

Here is another way to reach 10!

✦✦✦ + ✦✦✦✦✦✦✦ = **10** sea stars

Change the order of the numbers. Add them again. How many sea stars now?

✦✦✦✦✦✦✦ + ✦✦✦ = How many sea stars?

Sea turtles wait.

It's bath time on the reef. Striped cleaner fish clean the sea turtle. They eat dead skin and stuff that grows on the shell. Soon the turtle's <u>flippers</u>, <u>scales</u>, and tail are clean. **Next!**

sea turtles

There are still more ways to get to 10. Four sea turtles have their bath. Then six more. How many clean sea turtles does that make?

Five new sea turtles swim in. Five more join. How many more sea turtles are ready for a bath?

Jellyfish drift along.

Ten, twenty, or more
float. The water pulls
them through the sea.
They spin and dance.
Moon jellies eat small
eggs, fish, and shrimp.

moon jellies

You can count by 10s by adding 10 each time.

$0 +$ 🪼🪼🪼🪼🪼🪼🪼🪼🪼🪼 $= 10$

$10 +$ 🪼🪼🪼🪼🪼🪼🪼🪼🪼🪼 $= 20$

$20 +$ 🪼🪼🪼🪼🪼🪼🪼🪼🪼🪼 $= 30$

$30 +$ 🪼🪼🪼🪼🪼🪼🪼🪼🪼🪼 $=$ How many jellyfish?

fish

Fish swim in a school.

They stay safe together.
Forty, fifty, or more show up.
Now they look like one big fish!

Try It!

You can start at any number and count by 10s. Let's try it. Count by 10s starting from 40.

40 + [fish] = How many fish?

reef squid

Squid move as quiet as a whisper.

Closer and closer. Then one strikes. The squid grabs a shrimp with two long tentacles. Then it holds on to the shrimp with its eight arms as it eats.

Try It!

Counting by 10s works no matter what you count. See for yourself.

50 + = How many squid?

Manta rays swim in a row.

They leave the reef to hunt for
fish way down below.

manta rays

Deeper and deeper they go.

Try It!

You can count down by 10s, too. Start at 60. Count down 10 at a time.

60

50

40

30

20

10

Ten manta rays swim away. How many are left?

One dolphin plays alone.

Squeak, squeak. Its <u>pod</u> is coming. A pod is a group. How many dolphins in a pod? It depends. Most pods have from five to fifteen dolphins. This one has 10.

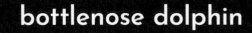
bottlenose dolphin

You can get to 100 by counting dolphin pods of 10. It's easy.

0

10

20

30

40

50

60

70

80

90

100!

Leap! Splash!

Tens of dolphins race to swim and play in the waves.

Try It! Activities

Here are counting activities kids can do to take the fun beyond the pages of this book.

SHARK SLEEPOVER (pages 4–5)

Some sharks who live in reefs sleep piled on top of each other in small caves. A baby shark is about as long as your leg. Figure out how many baby sharks can fit under your bed or desk. Use your legs or stuffed toys the size of your legs to approximately measure your bed or desk. This will help you figure it out. Where else could 10 sharks fit in your house? How about 20?

ROOM FOR GIANTS (pages 8–9)

A giant clam can be 40 inches (about 1 m) wide or wider! That's as long as your arms held wide open. Use your arms or a long-sleeved shirt to figure out how many giant clams could fit on your bed or couch. Could 10 giant clams fit in your room?

HOME, STINGING HOME (pages 10–11)

Clownfish live in small groups in a sea anemone. They chatter a lot. Clownfish make click, grunt, and pop sounds. Talk like a clownfish. How would it sound if you counted to 10 with grunts? Now count to 50 by 10s using pops. Count to 100 by 10s with clicks.

ONE HUNDRED BABY TURTLES (pages 14–15)

Ten baby sea turtles could fit on this page. How many pages would it take to hold 100 baby sea turtles? Count by 10s.

JELLYFISH BALLET (pages 16–17)

Jellyfish float and sway with the sea. The water pushes and pulls them. Become a jellyfish. Sway, twirl, and dance as if you were underwater. As you dance, count to 10 and start again.

FISH FUN (pages 18–19)

Many reef fish swim in schools. Use your hands to count 50 reef fish. Hold up both hands to show all 10 fingers. Open and close your hands each time you count up and down by 10s. Say this chant to help you count.

10, 20, 30, 40, 50 fish.

Oh no. There's a hungry whale.

50, 40, 30, 20, 10 tails swish!

MANTA MATH (pages 22–23)

Manta rays flap their fins to swim. Flap your arms like a manta ray. From tip to tip, a manta ray's fins are the length of a car! Estimate how many manta rays could "park" on your street or in a nearby parking lot. BONUS: Two manta rays could sit on top of a school bus. How many buses will you need to give 10 manta rays a ride to school? (Hint: Count by 2s.)

CRUISING SPEED (pages 24–25)

Dolphins move their tails up and down to swim. A dolphin swimming slowly pumps its tail about 20 times in 15 seconds. Count how many steps you take in 15 seconds. Have someone time you.

Glossary

clam (klam) A shellfish, often used as food, that has two tightly closed shells, which are hinged together.

flipper (FLIP-ur) One of the broad, flat limbs that sea animals such as sea turtles, seals, whales, and dolphins use when they swim.

jellyfish (JEL-ee-fish) A sea creature with a soft body and long, trailing tentacles that can sting.

manta ray (MAN-tuh ray) A kind of large fish that lives in the sea. Currently, there are two known kinds of manta rays, the giant manta ray and the reef manta ray.

pod (pahd) A group of certain kinds of sea animals, as in a pod of whales or dolphins. When several pods swim together, it is called a herd.

reef (reef) A strip of rock, sand, or coral close to the surface of the ocean or another body of water.

scale (skale) One of the thin, flat, overlapping pieces of hard skin that cover the body and shell of a sea turtle.

sea anemone (see uh-NEM-uh-nee) A sea animal with a body shaped like a tube and a mouth opening that is surrounded by tentacles that sting.

tentacle (TEN-tuh-kuhl) One of the long, flexible limbs of some animals, such as jellyfish, octopuses, squid, and sea anemones. These animals use their tentacles to move and to feel and grasp things.

Try It!

Answers

PAGE 7 10 sharks

PAGE 8
1 + 9 = 10 clams

PAGE 11
2 + 8 = 10 clownfish

PAGE 13
7 + 3 = 10 sea stars

PAGE 15
4 + 6 = 10 sea turtles

5 + 5 = 10 sea turtles

PAGE 17 40 jellyfish

PAGE 19 50 fish

PAGE 21 60 squid

PAGE 23 0 manta rays

Index

Page numbers in **bold** indicate illustrations.

ABOUT THE AUTHOR

Ruth A. Musgrave lives on land, but her heart is in the sea. She shares her love of animals and nature through her books and articles. She is the author of thirty-five books, including *Mission: Shark Rescue* and BBC Earth's *Do You Know? Animal Sounds*.